CLEOPATRA

Leaders of the Ancient World

CLEOPATRA

ZOE LOWERY AND

JULIAN MORGAN

Published in 2017 by The Rosen Publishing Group, Inc.
29 East 21st Street, New York, NY 10010

First Edition

Library of Congress Cataloging-in-Publication Data

Names: Lowery, Zoe, author. | Morgan, Julian, 1958– author.
Title: Cleopatra / Zoe Lowery and Julian Morgan.
Description: New York : Rosen Publishing, 2017. | Series: Leaders of the ancient world | Includes bibliographical references and index.
Identifiers: LCCN 2016024153 | ISBN 9781508172543 (library bound)
Subjects: LCSH: Cleopatra, Queen of Egypt, –30 B.C.—Juvenile literature. | Queens—Egypt—Biography—Juvenile literature. | Egypt—History—332-30 B.C.—Juvenile literature. | Rome—History—Republic, 265-30 B.C.—Juvenile literature.
Classification: LCC DT92.7 .L69 2017 | DDC 932/.021092 [B] —dc23
LC record available at https://lccn.loc.gov/2016024153

Manufactured in China

CONTENTS

INTRODUCTION

Egypt's history would never be the same after Macedon's Alexander the Great reached its borders in 332 BCE. He became the new pharaoh and was confirmed in his post by a royal oracle. A great new city was founded at the mouth of the Nile that bore his name: Alexandria. Macedonian Egypt was an important part of Alexander's swiftly expanding empire, but from this time on its rulers would be Greeks, not Egyptians. After Alexander died in 323 BCE, his huge empire was split up into sections that could be more easily administered by local rulers. Egypt was awarded to Alexander's former general Ptolemy, and a new dynasty of pharaohs began.

The Greek Ptolemies would rule Egypt for the next 300 years, and the last of them would be Cleopatra. She is often referred to as Cleopatra VII, because she was the seventh person with this name to have become queen of Egypt. Her very name means "Famous in Her Father," and her full name was Cleopatra VII Thea Philopator, which means "Cleopatra the Father-Loving Goddess."

Cleopatra is one of history's most famous leaders. She has been the subject of countless

Cleopatra's rule would be so notable (or notorious, according to some) that it would inspire innumerable books, plays, operas, ballets, and movies.

books, plays, operas, ballets, and movies through the centuries. She was as smart as she was charming and alluring. And Cleopatra did not hesitate to use all of her talents to her full advantage throughout her career. According to *National Geographic* magazine's Chip Brown, Greek historian Plutarch described the notorious ruler as not "the sort that would astound those who saw her; interaction with her was captivating, and her appearance, along with her persuasiveness in discussion and her character that accompanied every interchange, was stimulating. Pleasure also came with the tone of her voice, and her tongue was like a many-stringed instrument."

Primary sources for Cleopatra consist of two types. Written evidence comes from a number of ancient accounts, the main sources being that of Dio Cassius in his *Roman History* and that of the historian Plutarch in his *Life of Mark Antony*. There is also a wealth of archaeological evidence, in Rome and in Egypt especially, but evidence exists in other outposts of the empire as well. Also important are inscriptions and coinage, which provide valuable portraiture as well as additional information.

The search for her final resting place has been a quandary for years. Unfortunately, as Brown writes, "Earthquakes, tidal waves, rising seas, subsiding ground, civil conflicts, and the unsentimental recycling of building stones have destroyed the ancient quarter where for three centuries Cleopatra and her ancestors lived. Most of the glory that was ancient Alexandria now lies about 20 feet underwater." Several hopeful excavations have, to date, come up empty handed.

CHAPTER 1

PAVING THE WAY FOR CLEOPATRA

As the country was handed over to General Ptolemy, Egypt played an important role in the Mediterranean economy. Alexandria was a center for trade in glass, papyrus, wool, and other goods. The city had a medical school, a world famous library, and the Pharos lighthouse. Its architecture was much admired, and it was a cultural center without equal. Egypt's agricultural wealth and its industry made it a rich and powerful nation, but it still had to be administered carefully by its rulers, who controlled the production and the prices of many commodities.

The Ptolemies created a strong bureaucratic system of control across the land, and it became normal for the Greek rulers, wearing Macedonian felt hats and high boots, to treat the native Egyptian inhabitants as their slaves. Not one of the

Greek kings or queens even bothered to learn the Egyptian language until Cleopatra came to rule. The land of Egypt suffered great internal strife, with a growing divide between Greek and Egyptian peoples, as well as between Alexandria and the rest of the country. The Ptolemies even employed eunuchs in top positions so that there would be no chance of them having their own successors. They kept themselves separate from their subjects, and adopted the ancient Egyptian royal custom of marrying their own brothers and sisters.

The early Ptolemies extended Egypt's territory to include the island of Cyprus, Cyrenaica (which occupied much of modern-day Libya), Syria, and Phoenicia. Farther north, the Egyptians gained some cities and lands within Asia Minor and Greece, as their empire gradually grew in size. The first three kings, each called Ptolemy, were responsible for this, and it was only after the death of Ptolemy III in 222 BCE that the empire began to decrease in size again. The early days of expansion were seen as a kind of golden age for the dynasty, which later rulers dreamed of recreating.

At the same time that Egypt's rule was contracting, however, the influence of Rome was

The Pharos lighthouse, along with a library and a medical center, was just one of Alexandria's major cultural and architectural marvels.

growing in the central Mediterranean. The two states would have to learn to live together, though a mistrust existed between Greeks and Romans that would make this difficult to achieve. The capture of Greece by Rome in 146 BCE marked a time of change, as the Romans relentlessly came to control more and more of the lands around Italy.

In 80 BCE, the Egyptians had a new king, Ptolemy XII, also called Ptolemy Auletes, meaning "the flute player." In typical fashion, he married his sister, Cleopatra V, and he began a quest to establish an arrangement with the Romans that would secure his and Egypt's futures. He had six children, of whom the first three were probably born to Cleopatra V and the last three to another wife. They were Cleopatra VI, Berenike IV, Cleopatra VII, Arsinoe IV, Ptolemy XIII, and Ptolemy XIV. Cleopatra VII was born in 70 or possibly 69 BCE. Each one of these children was to become a ruler at some stage in his or her life, and most of them met unfortunate deaths. This was a time of great change and disturbance.

THE EGYPT–ROME ALLIANCE

Rome's desire was to control Egypt. As the Roman Empire began to grow in size, naturally, the number of mouths it had to feed increased as well. Egyptian grain would help considerably, though if this could be secured without force or coercion, it would be a much more attractive arrangement.

The Roman general Pompey the Great had won several eastern lands for Rome in recent years,

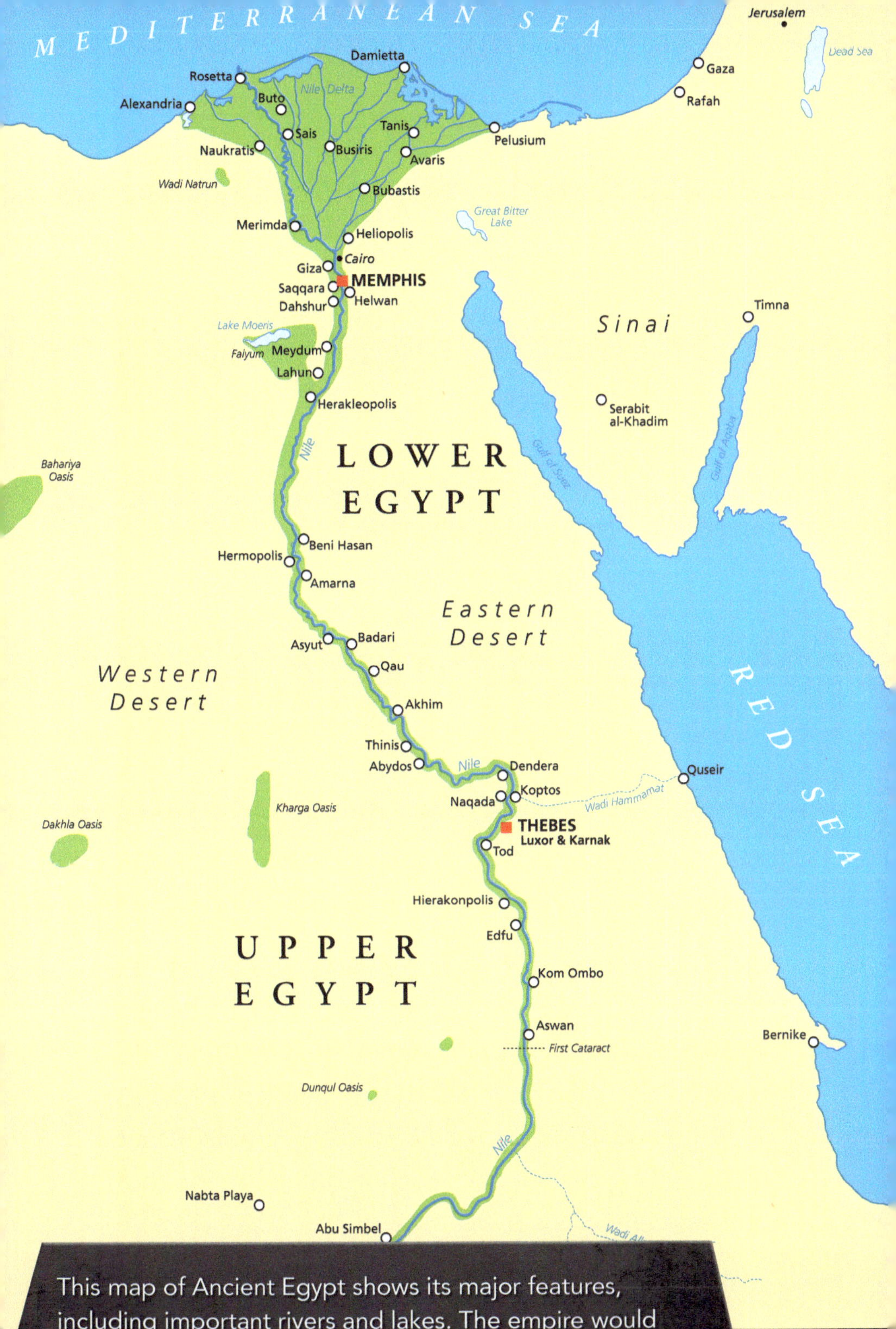

This map of Ancient Egypt shows its major features, including important rivers and lakes. The empire would eventually decrease in size.

THE INUNDATION

Each year the great river Nile, which flows from south to north across the country, would rise up as the melting snows from the southern mountains filled the river. This huge, annual flood was called the Inundation.

As the country was handed over to General Ptolemy, Egypt played a very important role in the Mediterranean economy. The flood left a great deposit of mud and organic matter across the floor of the valley, and when the water levels finally receded, the farmers could sow their crops in the newly fertile soil. Egypt's harvests were huge, and its grain was exported across the known world, producing tremendous wealth for the Egyptians.

including much of Syria in 63 BCE, which was previously controlled by another Macedonian dynasty, known as the Seleucids. Pompey the Great had also reduced the land of Judea to a dependent province of Rome, which had resulted in considerable resentment among the Jewish people who had made their homes there.

By 60 BCE, Pompey had formed an alliance, often called the first triumvirate, with two other leading Romans, Julius Caesar and Marcus Licinius Crassus. There were arguments for and against adding Egypt to Rome's growing empire, but for the time being it seemed best to leave it under its own control, especially if the local Egyptian rulers were pro-Roman.

Caesar had his eye on establishing a new province called Gaul in what is now France and Belgium, while the other two triumvirs kept a tight rein on the rest of the empire. Now was not the time to attack Egypt. Instead, the triumvirs agreed to accept the sum of 6,000 talents from Ptolemy XII, so that he could be recognized as a friend and ally of the Roman people.

The sum of 6,000 talents was a lot of money back in ancient days. It is not easy to say exactly how much it would amount to in modern terms, but it has been suggested that it may have been almost all of the profits from one year's trading in Egypt.

Ptolemy XII, although keen to keep Roman support, was unable to pay the money in one transaction, so he borrowed it, knowing that he would

Julius Caesar.

have to repay it later from his country's revenues. He kept the loan quiet in Egypt, waiting for a good moment to tell his people. The money came from a Roman banker Gaius Rabirius Postumus.

In 58 BCE, the Romans decided to take over Cyprus. This island had been part of the Ptolemies' empire for more than 200 years. It was governed at that time by the brother of Ptolemy XII, who committed suicide when he lost his kingdom. The loss of the island was keenly felt in Egypt, and the people were by now fully aware of the king's loan from Rabirius, as Ptolemy had raised taxes to start paying it off. As a consequence, Ptolemy fell from popular favor and had to leave Egypt suddenly. He went to Rome, possibly accompanied by his daughter Cleopatra VII.

In the king's absence, the new joint rulers of Egypt were his daughters Cleopatra VI and Berenike IV. This was customary, though normally joint rulers consisted of one male and one female member of the Ptolemy household.

Ptolemy XII found his claims for assistance in Rome well supported, as Rabirius put pressure on Pompey and Caesar to help restore him to his throne. If he was not returned to power, the money owed would not be repaid, so there were powerful arguments for supporting Ptolemy. His daughters, meanwhile, sought to accuse him of improper practices and sent 100 people to Rome to testify against him. Many of these witnesses were murdered as soon as they set foot in Italy, and the case against him was never presented. These acts demonstrate his ruthlessness as well as his ability to mobilize help in a foreign country.

As Ptolemy XII awaited an outcome, he left Rome and made his way eastward to Ephesus, which was located on the west coast of modern Turkey. Here he made a deal with Aulus Gabinius, the governor of the new Roman province of Syria, who agreed to restore him to his throne by force in return for a fee of 10,000 talents. One of Gabinius's young officers, Mark Antony, persuaded him to accept the deal. This payment, combined with the earlier loan from Rabirius, would help secure Ptolemy's future. He knew that he would continue to receive support from Rome if he owed so much money to its people. Without his presence, the debt would not be repaid.

At this point, Cleopatra VI mysteriously disappeared from the scene. Berenike IV needed

Ptolemy XII.

a coruler, so she sought a husband. She first fixed on a man called Seleucus, probably from the fallen dynasty in Syria, but she was so disappointed in him that she ordered him to be strangled to death three days after he arrived in Alexandria. She then arranged a marriage with Archelaus, a prince from Pontus, the area south of the Black Sea. He had been a friend of Pompey the Great, supporting him on his campaigns and extending hospitality to his lieutenant Mark Antony.

However, Archelaus soon died when Gabinius led his forces into Egypt. Antony saw to it that his former host received an honorable burial, which may have been when he met Cleopatra for the first time, though their famous love affair would not begin for many years to come.

This relief shows Cleopatra VII with her father Ptolemy XII and the goddess Isis. Cleopatra was only nineteen when she began her rule.

In the meantime, Antony's decent behavior probably earned him some popularity among the Alexandrians. Ptolemy XII was restored to his throne in 55 BCE. Gabinius and Rabirius together tried to extract as much wealth from Egypt as they could, in return for their loans, but this behavior only resulted in their being forced out of Egypt for their unreasonable conduct. Gabinius went into exile, and Rabirius received a pledge from Julius Caesar that he would get his money back for him. The army of Gabinius was retained by Ptolemy XII, who used it as a mercenary force in his own country. Berenike IV was killed on her father's orders for her treachery to him.

CLEOPATRA ON THE THRONE

Because Egypt's dynasty was customarily ruled by a pair, Ptolemy XII needed a coruler. In 51 BCE he decided that his daughter Cleopatra VII should rule with him. At the young age of only 19 years, Cleopatra had probably never ruled before, and her time working with her father was brief. Later that very year, Ptolemy XII died, but his daughter had already learned a lot, even in the short time in which they ruled together. Throughout her reign, Cleopatra sought to restore Egypt's former glory. Like her father, she recognized that Rome was increasingly in control. The road to victory and stability required that Rome be a strong supporting partner with Egypt. Otherwise, Egypt's name would fade into obscurity as one of Rome's plethora of provinces. And so Cleopatra VII ascended to the throne facing some serious challenges.

CHAPTER 2

CLEOPATRA AND CAESAR

In a nod to the Ptolemies' custom, Cleopatra consented to rule together with Ptolemy XIII, her younger brother. It was a complicated situation. Ptolemy XIII had priority over her, simply because he was male; however, because at ten years old the boy was still a minor, a council of advisors represented him. The council and Cleopatra had some major differences of opinion, such as her belief that Egypt needed Rome's support. Not long into her reign, Cleopatra left Alexandria when matters got heated with the advisers.

CLEOPATRA'S FIRST CLASHES

In those days, the Egyptian and Greek subjects were so vastly different that the two groups were required to crown their pharaohs. Unlike some of

Ptolemy XIII was only ten years old when he began to share power as coruler with his sister, Cleopatra VII.

her predecessors, Cleopatra had taken the trouble to communicate with her Egyptian subjects and make friends beyond Alexandria, which meant that she had support beyond the Greek communities. This allowed her to rely on friends in the south of the country, called Upper Egypt, when disagreements broke out.

One major clash between Cleopatra and Ptolemy XIII's council occurred when Syria's Roman governor, Marcus Calpurnius Bibulus, sent his two sons to Alexandria to ask for the assistance of the former army of Gabinius, which was still in the pay of the Ptolemies.

Bibulus was under attack by the Parthians, who threatened to overwhelm Syria, and so his priority was defending Roman territory. His two sons were murdered, however, as the soldiers in Egypt had no desire to go to Syria or to help the Romans who appeared to have entirely abandoned the cause. Cleopatra arrested the individuals responsible and sent them to Bibulus to deal with, who in turn sent them to Rome for justice at the hands of the Senate. This caused great resentment in Alexandria, and it may have been the decisive moment in the split from Ptolemy XIII's supporters, who would have resented not only what happened, but the underlying reasons for it—that is, Cleopatra's policy of giving way to Rome.

There may have been other problems, too, such as crop failures in 50 and 49 BCE, and a ban by Ptolemy XIII's council on the movement of grain between different parts of Egypt, perhaps in a move to block supplies to Cleopatra.

JULIUS VERSUS POMPEY: ROME'S WAR

Egypt's problems were minor in comparison to what was happening elsewhere. A great civil war was going on across the Roman world between the forces of Julius Caesar and those of his former colleague, Pompey the Great. In early 49 BCE, Cnaeus Pompeius, Pompey's son, came to ask for Egyptian help on his father's behalf in this struggle, and he was warmly received by Ptolemy's council, who gave him some 500 soldiers from the former army of Gabinius along with 60 ships. Furthermore, grain was sent to Pompey's base of operations in Dyrrhachium (modern Durazzo in Albania), and Pompey was chosen as Ptolemy XIII's guardian.

The boy Ptolemy XIII became embroiled in a large-scale conflict on the side of the man who was destined to lose, while his sister, Cleopatra, had managed to avoid any kind of partisanship. She may have been in the territory of the Nabataean Arabs by now, in modern Jordan. She was probably working out how to raise support for herself in a bid to return to Alexandria, not realizing at the time that her best chance lay in the failure of her opponents at home to back the right contender.

After a major defeat at Pharsalus, Greece, in 48 BCE, Pompey himself came to Egypt for support, because he had received such generous help there the previous year. However, instead of receiving help, he was murdered by Achillas, a Greek officer in the Egyptian army, and by Lucius Septimius, a member of the former army of Gabinius. They came to pick him up in a rowboat and stabbed him as he came on board. The reasons for the assassination are unclear, but the leading minister of Egypt, Pothinus, who had been chairman of Ptolemy's council of advisors, seems to have been responsible. Pothinus did not want to see the conflict between Pompey and Caesar continue on Egyptian soil, especially given the political

CAESAR ARRIVES

Caesar came to Egypt not far behind Pompey. He arrived in Alexandria with ten ships and about 4,000 soldiers, a negligible force. He was given Pompey's head and signet ring on his arrival, which must surely have disgusted him. Indeed, it soon became obvious that he would find it hard to get along with Pothinus, Achillas, or Ptolemy XIII. Caesar had purchased the Egyptian debt from Rabirius, and now he wanted to see it paid back to him.

He made a critical mistake on his arrival in the city by wearing the robes of a Roman consul and having attendants carry the emblems of his authority. The Alexandrians were determined not to capitulate to the Roman oppressor, whoever he might be. They roited against him.

Caesar met with Ptolemy XIII, and was perhaps surprised to see Cleopatra arrive in the palace at Alexandria at the same time. The story is that she was smuggled in by sea from the east and brought to Caesar in a roll of bedding, concealed from her brother's supporters. Caesar judged her more trustworthy than Ptolemy XIII or Pothinus, and they became lovers.

problems between his young king and Cleopatra. A cowardly act of violence seemed a good way out for Egypt, though it would guarantee no future deals with Caesar himself, who was a fearsome figure at that time.

In the months that followed Caesar's arrival, Cleopatra saw him as the potential savior for the Ptolemies' dynasty and the only man with sufficient power in Rome to secure the future of her house. Caesar probably saw her as the only guarantee that the money loaned by Rabirius would ever be returned. He also recognized that Egypt and Rome could coexist within a carefully contrived framework. Caesar, like Mark Antony later on, saw that the Roman habit of crushing foreign rulers was not necessarily the best way to achieve political stability. He must also have been attracted to Cleopatra physically, and her reputation as a seducer of men must have been justified in part. We are told that she was not especially beautiful, but that she had considerable charm. There are no reasons at all to believe that she was promiscuous, as we know only of her love affairs

Whatever her feelings for him, Cleopatra may have viewed her relationship with Caesar as a means to raise some much needed funds for her country.

with two men, Caesar and Antony. Certainly she was able to bewitch other men to some extent, and this must have been the result of her personality rather than her looks, if we can believe the accounts told at the time. Many portraits depict her with a rather large, hooked nose. At the time of her relationship with Caesar she was probably 22 years old, and he was 52.

When Ptolemy XIII first heard of Caesar's affair with his sister, he tore the diadem from his head and rushed out into the streets of Alexandria in a rage. Pothinus must have been similarly furious and the rioting in Alexandria continued. The Egyptian army was called back to the city, as Caesar sent for reinforcements from Syria and Asia Minor. He sent representatives to meet with Achillas, the Greek army commander, but they were killed. The palace where Caesar resided was held under siege as he racked his brains to decide what to do next. He managed to bring the royal brother and sister together, keeping Ptolemy XIII under lock and key. Then he awarded the island of Cyprus, which had been acquired by Rome 10 years earlier, to the Egyptian family dynasty, appointing sister Arsinoe IV and brother Ptolemy XIV as its joint rulers. By giving it back to the Ptolemies, Caesar was attempting to gain some support in Egypt and to split up the Ptolemy brothers and sisters into manageable units.

Caesar now made a bold raid, attacking and destroying the Egyptian fleet in the great harbor at Alexandria. Cleopatra must have had mixed views about this, as she saw her ships go up in flames, but she continued to trust in her lover. She must have been even more concerned to see the flames spread to her famous library. Many rare books were destroyed in the flames, though it is unclear whether the library itself was burned or the area nearby, where books were awaiting transportation.

Caesar made the Theater of Dionysus his center of operations, and he gradually gained control of the city. The great Pharos lighthouse was taken from the rioters, but Caesar was cut off on the causeway leading to it. From there he had to swim to his ships in order to escape.

Arsinoe IV had not been able to go to Cyprus yet, and now she escaped from the palace, causing further concern and more widespread rioting. Her minister, the eunuch Ganymedes, accompanied her to the rioters and she was proclaimed queen.

Pothinus, under house arrest in the palace, sent a message to Achillas indicating his support for Arsinoe IV, but this was intercepted, and Pothinus was killed on Caesar's orders. In the meantime, Achillas was killed too, probably by supporters of his enemy Ganymedes. The lack of coordinated resistance among the Egyptians certainly helped Caesar's cause. He now proceeded to release Ptolemy XIII, who took over command of the rebellious forces from Ganymedes. In March 47 BCE, reinforcements for Caesar arrived under the leadership of Mithridates of Pergamum, a Roman-controlled city in Asia Minor. The troops included soldiers from Judea, whose people had hated Pompey and were therefore well disposed to help Caesar in his difficulties. The final battle took place out-

According to legend, Cleopatra choreographed a surprising and dramatic entrance for Caesar by way of a roll of bedding or carpet.

side the city and Caesar reentered Alexandria as a conqueror. Ptolemy XIII was drowned in the Nile.

LOVE AND POWER

At the end of the Alexandrian war, Caesar was more determined than ever to make a deal with Cleopatra to secure control of Egypt. He had struggled hard to win back Alexandria for his young mistress, and now he wanted to see the reward for those efforts. Cleopatra was pregnant, and Caesar must have thought about her having his son, who might one day rule Egypt. If this could happen, the future loyalty of Egypt to Rome would surely be guaranteed. Caesar knew that the great wealth of the country placed it in a unique category, and it would be hard to find any Roman governor honest enough to be entrusted with its administration. So he took various steps to secure the future for Cleopatra and her country. His vision was shared by the queen, who continued to promote peace with Rome, as her father had done before her.

It was at this time, 47 BCE, that Caesar and Cleopatra went on a cruise up the river Nile together, though the exact details of this trip are hard to establish. It seems that the queen wanted to show Caesar her country, and he wanted the Egypitan people to see him with her, as the guarantor of their safety. This was more than just a simple cruise. Caesar took 400 ships with him. He made various settlements before leaving, which included appointing 12-year-old Ptolemy XIV as Cleopatra's coruler. This was certainly just a token gesture, as Cleopatra was clearly the person in charge, and she wanted no further factional disputes or problems from advisory councils. Ptolemy was given full responsibility for Cyprus, and it may have been Cleopatra's intention to occupy him with the island to keep him out of her way. Arsinoe IV was shipped off to Rome under arrest.

Caesar now restored to Judea the status it had enjoyed before Pompey had made it a Roman province, making it a client kingdom of Rome. This meant that it could keep its own ruler as its king, provided that the government complied with Rome's will. This restoration was a reward for the help Judea had provided to Caesar in overcoming the Alexandrian rioters. When he left Egypt in the summer of 47 BCE, Caesar also left three of his legions behind as a security force, comprising about 15,000 men. The legions could protect Cleopatra and her family from any further problems that might arise from her people, or they could act as a restraining force if the Egyptians tried to go it alone. Caesar left an ex-slave called Rufio in charge of this force. It is odd that he did not leave someone with a more elevated rank in charge, but perhaps this is a reminder that he was afraid to entrust a command in Egypt to an ambitious Roman officer who could become corrupted by its wealth.

After Caesar's departure from Egypt, Cleopatra must have felt much more secure than at any moment since first becoming queen in 51 BCE. She could now control her own land and her own destiny, though clearly she had chosen to follow Caesar's star. Her son was born later in 47 BCE, and he was commonly known as Caesarion, meaning "little Caesar." Her own name for him was Ptolemy Caesar, which stressed his family connections to both Rome and Egypt. There is some dispute about his parentage, but it is generally accepted that he was Caesar's son in fact as well as in name.

Caesar went on to crush the last of Pompey's followers at the battle of Thapsus, in modern Tunisia, in April of 46 BCE. He then returned to Rome to

The infamous lovers Antony and Cleopatra are depicted in William Shakespeare's play of the same name, as well as in many other mediums.

celebrate four triumphs (parades) in short succession. One celebrated the victory in the Alexandrian war, where Arsinoe IV was included in the parade, bound in chains. She was then sent off to Ephesus, in modern Turkey, to be held a virtual prisoner at the Temple of Artemis. Her advisor, Ganymedes, was also paraded before the Romans before being killed for his part in opposing Caesar. Cleopatra came to Rome shortly afterward, as it would not have looked good for her to witness the disgrace of her own countrymen in Caesar's triumph. She stayed in one of his houses on the Janiculum Hill, where she was an honored guest. Her son, Caesarion, came with her, though neither one could have been exactly welcomed by Caesar's wife, Calpurnia. As tribute, Caesar had a golden statue of her placed in the Temple of Venus Genetrix (the symbolic mother of Rome) in a newly developed part of the Forum. This was a major mark of favor, conferring the status of a divinity on her in such a public place. Caesar was now emperor of Rome in all but name, though his official title was dictator, which he eventually adopted on a permanent basis. Before this, a dictator had been an elected official of the city, chosen to serve in times of crisis for a limited period of time, but Caesar had other ideas.

Later in the year 46 BCE, Caesar went on a campaign to Spain. Cleopatra may have returned to Egypt. Caesar's return to Rome in the following year saw them reunited, however, though in his will at that time he made no mention of Cleopatra or his supposed natural son Caesarion. His own authority and position in Rome came into question as leading senators began to detest his arrogance and unconstitutional usurpation of power. Cleopatra's presence in the city probably did not help. There was gossip about Caesar's wife, and it seemed as if Caesar thought himself above the normal conventions of society. He was regarded as a threat to the

Although some question whether or not Caesarion was actually Caesar's son, it is generally accepted that he was.

continued existence of the republic, the system of government that guaranteed free Roman citizens a voice in the rule of Rome.

On March 15, 44 BCE, what was essentially the night before leaving for Parthia on a new campaign that Cleopatra planned to support with her vast fortune, tragedy struck. On the steps of Pompey's Theater, 23 conspirators stabbed Caesar. Aware of the repercussions and pandemonium that would certainly result from her lover's murder, Cleopatra quickly fled Rome.

CHAPTER 3

GODS AND RULERS

Following Caesar's murder, a struggle for power pitched Rome into another civil war. Central to this power struggle was the foundation of a second triumvirate in 43 BCE formed by Mark Antony, Octavian, and Marcus Aemilius Lepidus. Each man in this trio wanted to punish Caesar's assassins—primarily Marcus Junius Brutus and Gaius Cassius Longinus—while increasing his own power with no concern for the others unless it was to his own benefit.

Meanwhile, Cleopatra opted to bide her time safely in Egypt. Whomever emerged as victor would thus win her support. Although she thought all three could claim Caesar's position, only time would tell who would win it. Mark Antony, a tremendously talented general, had an excellent chance.

Caesarion, also known as Ptolemy Caesar, as his mother called him, became co-ruler with her after Caesar's assassination.

Then there was Octavian, named in Caesar's will as his main heir and already showing great political promise. Finally, her own son Caesarion could claim direct descent from the dictator. One of Cleopatra's first actions when she returned to Egypt was to engineer the death of her brother and coruler, Ptolemy XIV. By doing this, she elevated Caesarion to the position of coruler. Although he was still very much a child, perhaps not even three years old, this boosted her hopes for the continuation of an independent Egypt, while ensuring that she could retain full control over the monarchy.

Cleopatra was approached by envoys from Caesar's assassin Cassius, who sought protection and support for his cause in the East. He had come to Syria after Publius Cornelius Dolabella arrived to take control of the province as its new governor. Dolabella had been one of Caesar's officers, and now he had to remove Cassius before taking up his new post. He too asked Cleopatra for help, and she was uncertain which way to turn. In the end she sent Caesar's three legions from Egypt to join Dolabella, but he lost his claim to Syria and the armies went to Cassius. Thus, Cleopatra unwittingly helped Caesar's killers. Pressure continued to build on her, as Cassius had some support among her people in Alexandria.

In Cyprus, too, her governor Serapion supported Cassius, and Cleopatra was worried that if she did not back Cassius, there might be a move to bring Arsinoe IV, her sister, out of her forced retirement in Ephesus and back to the throne of Egypt. Yet she did not want to support the men who had killed her lover, and she must have been relieved when Cassius and Brutus met in Smyrna, modern Izmir on the west coast of Turkey. This took their war north, away from Egypt, and she decided now to back the side of the triumvirs Antony and Octavian, despite the fact that Serapion had gone over to Cassius's side. Cleopatra sailed from Alexandria with her fleet, but a combination of bad weather and personal sickness drove her back home before she was able to lend any concrete help.

The Battle of Philippi was fought in 42 BCE in northern Greece, and it was here that Antony and Octavian destroyed the forces of Caesar's killers, Brutus and Cassius, who both committed suicide. It appeared that Cleopatra had backed the right side, and Rome officially recognized her joint rule with Caesarion in Egypt as the triumvirs' reward for her support of Dolabella and themselves.

DIONYSUS MEETS ISIS

After the Battle of Philippi, Cleopatra awaited further developments from Rome. The arrangement between the triumvirs was that Octavian would look after matters in the western half of the empire, including Italy, whereas Mark Antony would take responsibility for the eastern half. In particular, Antony wanted to take up where Julius Caesar had left off, pursuing a campaign in the far eastern end of the empire against Parthia. This nation had previously caused difficulties many times in Rome's history, and Antony felt that there would be great glory in adding it to the list of Rome's client kingdoms.

Caesar had a special reason for wanting to go, which Antony felt he had inherited. Marcus Licinius Crassus, Caesar's colleague in the first triumvirate, had been dealt a crushing defeat there in 53 BCE, at Carrhae, modern Harran, Turkey, on the far side of the river Euphrates. The Roman con quest of Parthia was largely motivated by the desire for revenge for Crassus's humiliating loss.

The remains of a library in Ephesus, where Antony tackled the task of governing his part of the empire.

Antony now made his way to Ephesus, in Asia Minor, where he addressed the issues of governing his half of the empire. There were loyalties to be secured and armies to be paid, while supporters of Brutus and Cassius had to be punished. He had spent much of his time in the East and knew well what was expected there. Many of the cities he governed were Greek in origin, and Antony knew that their loyalty could be acquired in ways that would not necessarily bring results in the western half of the empire. At Ephesus, he was hailed as a new Dionysus by his Greek subjects, and he

ISIS ARRIVES

After hearing of Antony's assumption of the character of Dionysus, Cleopatra dressed herself as Aphrodite, the Greek goddess of love, and she sailed in her barge up the river Cydnus to meet him. The rear section of the boat was covered in beaten gold, while purple sails flapped in the breeze. The rowers had oars of silver, which dipped in the water gracefully to the sound of flutes playing.

Perfume wafted from the boat, as fans were used to cool the queen and spread the scents. Cleopatra herself lay back under a canopy of gold, while her attendants were dressed either as cupids, Aphrodite's children, or as the Graces. The mythological themes were entirely suggestive of what might come next. Antony was overwhelmed by his desire for the queen. Aphrodite had come to Dionysus.

The pharaohs of Egypt had been worshiped as divine for centuries, so it was entirely natural for Cleopatra to be seen as godlike. In ancient Egypt, many of the Greco-Roman gods were identified with local Egyptian gods and goddesses, so Dionysus was often regarded as equivalent to Osiris, the Egyptian god of rebirth. The Roman goddess Venus, or the Greek Aphrodite, was regarded as similar to Isis, a goddess whose worship in Egypt was extremely popular. Cleopatra represented herself as the personification of Isis on Earth to Antony's Osiris, in a way that her own people could appreciate and understand, too.

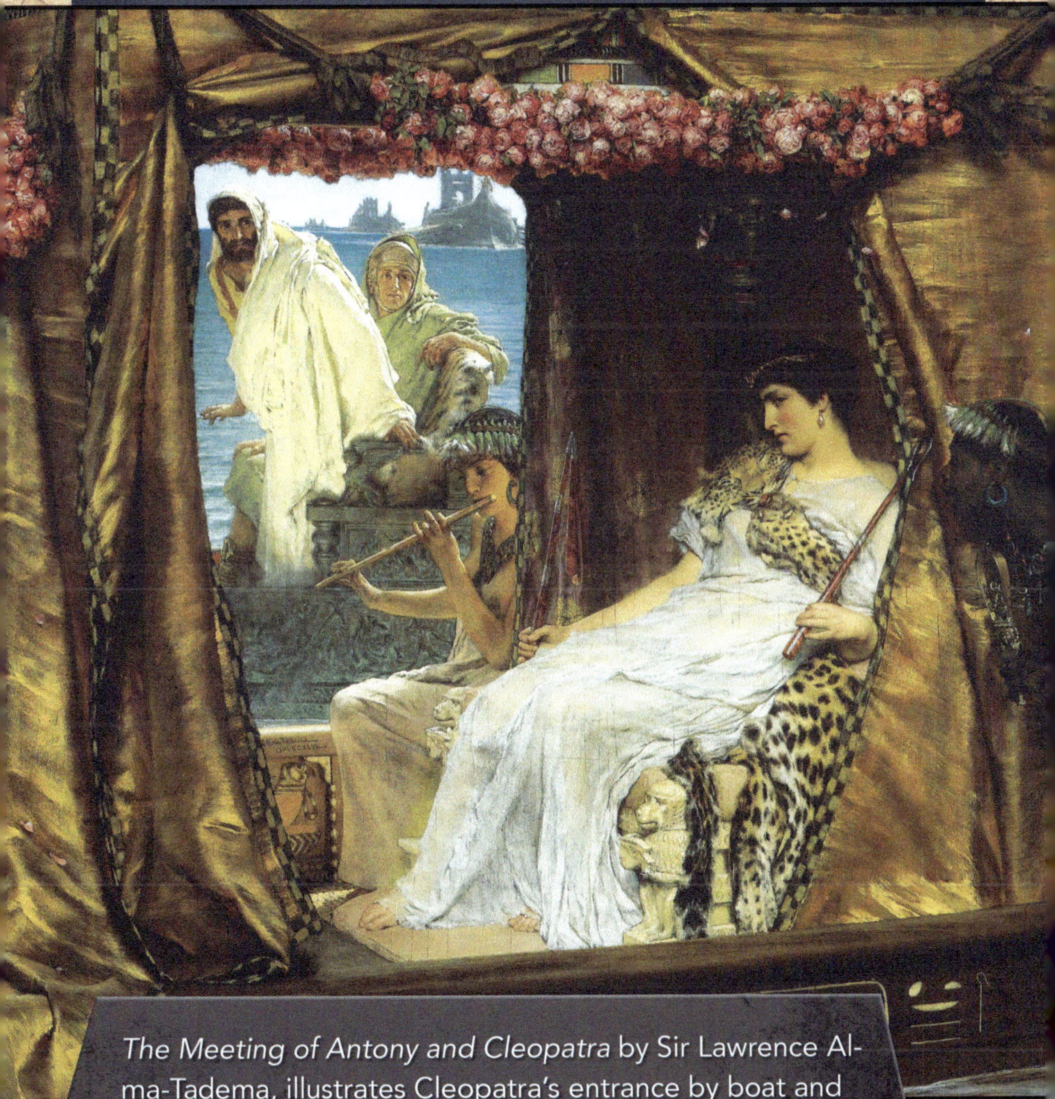

The Meeting of Antony and Cleopatra by Sir Lawrence Alma-Tadema, illustrates Cleopatra's entrance by boat and dressed as Aphrodite, goddess of love.

Cleopatra's Feast as illustrated by Johann Georg Platzer, depicts the dramatic dinner in Tarsus, which would prove to be just the first of many.

found that he rather enjoyed the idea of being divine. Dionysus was the Greek god of wine, celebration, and regeneration, and the bringer of joy. Antony liked his wine and certainly enjoyed parties, so this suited him well. Another role he assumed was that of Hercules, as he swaggered about in character, dressed up in a cloak with a long sword at his side.

Celebrations aside, Antony was making a serious assessment of how to conduct his campaign against Parthia, and Cleopatra soon came to his mind as someone who could help considerably. Egyptian finance would help, as would a reliable source of supplies, clothing, and provisions from Alexandria. He sent an officer and friend, Quintus Dellius, to summon her from Egypt, and in early 41 BCE the meeting took place at Tarsus, in Cilicia. The queen did not come immediately, but when she did it was done in style.

The meeting at Tarsus produced different results for Antony and Cleopatra. On the evening of their meeting she invited him to dinner, where he was utterly dazzled by the display of lighted torches and lamps. The banquet was wildly extravagant, the first of a series of such parties that would often go on until very late in the night. Antony's purpose was to find out whether Cleopatra had really supported Cassius's side in the civil war or not, and how she regarded events now. Would she give him the money to pay his troops and the other commodities he needed to bring off his Parthian campaign successfully? Could he rely on Egypt's cooperation now that the three legions left to guard it by Caesar had gone? How could he secure the queen's long-term loyalty?

Cleopatra, in turn, saw her chance to stabilize things in Egypt. She demanded that Arsinoe IV, her sister in Ephesus, be killed, on the grounds that she might have helped Cassius. Serapion, her disloyal governor in Cyprus, was to be killed, too. Cleopatra also became pregnant by Antony.

Antony agreed to accompany the queen back to Alexandria, to visit the city himself, and to secure their arrangements. Though he came as a private citizen, so as not to offend the Alexandrians, as Caesar had done seven years before.

Did the couple truly love one another at this point? It's unlikely. However, they seemed to revel in being together, and they lived a lavish life with wild and expensive parties. Once, to ensure the food was perfectly ready at the right time, they ordered that eight boars should be prepared, though the party was only made up of 12 people. Antony was rough and mirthful while Queen Cleopatra had a provocative lure. She hunted, played games, and drank right along with him. Meanwhile, both knew what they were doing, and both had their own separate plans for the future.

CHAPTER 4

EGYPT'S KINGDOM RESTORED

Antony needed to leave Cleopatra's side to travel back to his provinces in early 40 BCE. Two Parthian invasions had occurred there. Pacorus, son of the Parthian king, had spearheaded an assault on Syria, and Quintus Labienus, once a Roman general had attacked the province of Asia. Furthermore, Antony's own Syrian garrison had abandoned him.

There were also problems in Judea, where the Parthian invaders managed to overthrow the local ruler, Hyrcanus, after proceeding there from Syria. Antony moved swiftly to Asia, when more disturbing news came to him of a war in Italy that had been waged in his name but without his direct involvement. His brother, Lucius, and his wife, Fulvia, had stirred things up against Octavian, and a battle had been fought and lost in Perusia, modern Perugia in northern Italy. Antony knew that the problems in Italy were potentially more threatening to him than the Parthian menace, so he proceeded to meet with Fulvia, who had fled to Athens. He became angry with her, and she died soon afterward of illness.

In October of 40 BCE, Antony and Octavian met again at the port of Brundisium, modern Brindisi in southeast Italy, where they patched up the triumvirate and renegotiated their agreements. From this time on, Octavian would keep the Western empire, though Antony would be allowed to recruit soldiers in Italy, an important concession. Lepidus was given the province of Africa to govern, which roughly corresponds to modern-day Tunisia, and Antony was to continue to rule in the East, with a special commission to campaign in Parthia.

Lepidus was almost entirely sidelined now, and the triumvirate had become an arrangement between two major players, not three. However, the part of the agreement that would affect Cleopatra the most was the stipulation that Antony would marry Octavia, Octavian's sister. A marriage of convenience would secure the loyalty of both parties to the treaty, it was felt, and this would mean no more cavorting with the Egyptian queen.

It was hoped that Marc Antony's marriage to Octavia would mean he would cease his relationship with Cleopatra.

FRIENDS AND RIVALS

In the meantime, better news was coming from the East, where Antony's general, Publius Ventidius, was successfully driving back the Parthian invaders. He managed to drive Labienus out of Asia and to his death, and Pacorus too was defeated and killed. Antony took troops as far as the Euphrates to consolidate these gains, which were celebrated in Rome. Then, however, Octavian called him back to Italy, to a second summit meeting at Brundisium. Antony attended the meeting, but Octavian did not, and the two men fell out again. Octavia helped to patch things up and another meeting was called, this time in Tarentum, modern Taranto in southern Italy. As a result of this meeting in 37 BCE, Octavian promised Antony four legions of soldiers, 20,000 men, to help him in his Parthian campaign. Antony gave 120 ships to Octavian so he could subdue Sextus Pompeius, a son of Pompey the Great, who had set up a base in opposition in Sicily. The triumvirate was renewed until the end of 33 BCE, and the arrangements were secured by another promise of marriage, as Antyllus, Antony's eldest son by Fulvia, was betrothed to Octavian's

After summoning Antony back to Italy, Octavian did not even attend the arranged meeting, causing a new rift between the men.

daughter Julia. He was nine years old and she was seven, so this was a purely symbolic union.

ROMANCE AND NEGOTIATIONS

After the Treaty of Tarentum, Antony returned to the East, but he sent Octavia, his wife, back to Italy. Within a short space of time he was in Antioch, Syria, where he sent for Cleopatra, whom he had not seen now for three and a half years. He seems to have realized that Octavian's promises were an illusion, and that the promised four legions would never arrive. He knew that Cleopatra could give him all the wealth he needed to raise armies in the East, and probably saw this as a better and quicker way to get on with things. It would be best if his wife Octavia could not see at close hand what he was up to, as his dealings with his former mistress were likely to involve more than just politics. Indeed, within a short space of time the two were lovers again, though this time Cleopatra had managed to attach a set of conditions to her cooperation. We are told that she manipulated Antony by declaring extreme love for him. She ate so little that she wasted away, and she made sure that he saw

DISAPPOINTED HOPES

Cleopatra must have been disappointed to learn of Antony's union with Octavia. While she probably did not love Antony, she had just given birth to twins, his children, whom she had named Cleopatra and Alexander. She must have felt suddenly relieved when she heard of Fulvia's death, and perhaps a little optimistic that Antony would now return to her. The marriage with Octavia was a blow, therefore, and the pregnancy that followed cannot have been welcome news either. During this period, the Parthian invaders had come right up to Cleopatra's borders, and she must have had this on her mind, though the Parthians did not at any point actually threaten Egypt.

Cleopatra was instrumental in helping the Judean prince, Herod, escape to Rome to ask for help, but when he returned she was annoyed that he had been confirmed as the single ruler in the province by the triumvirs. Cleopatra had cast jealous eyes on Judea. She continued to maintain that Caesarion was Caesar's true heir, though there was little support elsewhere for this claim. News must have reached her of Antony and Octavia's happy life together, their house in Athens, and the birth of their daughter Antonia, but she had no choice but to bide her time in Alexandria and wait for the next opportunity to present itself to her.

her weeping. She did not want any chance of him returning to Octavia now.

All of her life, Cleopatra had sought the restoration of her family dynasty. The Ptolemies had ruled much of the coastal seaboard of the eastern Mediterranean, and she saw her chance now to re-create their old kingdom. The drawback was that she could only do this if the Romans gave the lands to her, as she had no intention at all of starting a military campaign. If Antony could promise her extended rule over his half of the Roman Empire, she in turn could regain the lost glories of her family. This was her condition for giving him what he needed, so he could achieve his aim of invading Parthia. By giving Cleopatra land, Antony felt that he was merely renegotiating how his portion

Katherine Hepburn plays a seductive Cleopatra in a performance of William Shakespeare's *Antony and Cleopatra.*

of the empire was ruled, so from his point of view there was nothing improper in doing this.

Cleopatra was given much of Syria and Ituraea, including what is now Lebanon. She also received land in modern Jordan, close to Israel, as well as land in Cilicia, in southern Asia Minor. These gifts meant that much of the old dynastic empire of the Ptolemies was restored. Just as important, the lands in question were all heavily wooded, so the agreement was for Cleopatra to build enough ships to protect Antony's empire in the eastern Mediterranean.

Antony did not let her have it all her own way, however. Cleopatra very much desired Judea and probably regretted the help she had recently given to its king, Herod. Antony remained firm on this point, however, and Judea stayed in Herod's possession, though he had to surrender some of its coastline, including the port of Joppa. Herod's only port was now that of Gaza, and he also had to give up several date groves near Jericho, which he agreed to rent back from Cleopatra. The queen persuaded Antony to give her some of the land of the Nabataean Arabs in modern-day Jordan. She took ownership of the southern Dead Sea area, where bitumen occurred naturally in the water. Bitumen was a valuable substance used for a wide variety of purposes, including medicinal ones. Herod agreed to act as intermediary between her and the local inhabitants, which she agreed to, though perhaps she resented his involvement.

Egypt, the lands around it, and their Roman rulers all had new a relationship now. To commemorate the occasion, Cleopatra's children by Antony were given new names: Alexander Helios, which means "the Sun," and Cleopatra Selene, which means "the Moon."

CHAPTER 5

RIDING ALONG THE ROAD TO RUIN

The last few years had brought significant changes to Parthia. King Phraates IV was the new ruler, who had murdered not only his father, but 30 of his brothers, too. Antony was no threat, as far as he was concerned.

HELP ARRIVES

Meanwhile, Antony completed preparations to launch his plans for an eastern expansion of Roman rule. After traveling north to Armenia, he headed south into Parthia where everything went wrong. Phraates, who was ready and waiting, forced Antony to retreat. The Parthians were waiting, and so heavily attacked him for 27 days, that he may have lost two-fifths of his army. As 36 BCE came to a close, he struggled to make it to Leuke

Kom, a small village on Asia Minor's west coast. He waited there for Cleopatra to join him with money and clothing he desperately needed for his troops. She even brought with her his new baby, whom she called Ptolemy Philadelphus. Cleopatra was apparently unfazed by Antony's significant military catastrophe.

In spring of 35 BCE, Octavian sent his sister to Athens to meet Antony and give him 2,000 men, as well as 70 ships. Clearly this was meant as an insult to Antony, as the original number of troops promised had been ten times this number. These 70 ships were all that were left out of the 120 that Antony had first given to Octavian. Antony reacted bluntly, telling Octavia to go home. He accompanied Cleopatra to Alexandria, where she continued to try to change his mind about giving Judea to Herod. A friend of hers called Alexandra was the mother of High Priest Aristobulus, whom Herod had killed, so Cleopatra demanded revenge. Antony called for Herod, heard his story, and decided to take no further action, though he did remove the port of Gaza from Herod's control.

Octavia.

ONWARD TO THE EAST

Antony and Cleopatra continued to plan campaigns in the East, as King Artavasdes of Media promised support if they attacked Parthia again. First, however, Antony invaded Armenia again, with Cleopatra accompanying him as far as the river Euphrates. Antony's campaign was a success this time, and he brought great wealth back to Alexandria, where he intended to celebrate the victory in style. Cleopatra had taken a long route home, visiting her newly acquired lands, including Damascus in Syria. She called in to see Herod in Judea, a meeting that was likely less than friendly.

In autumn of 34 BCE, the couple were together again in Alexandria. Antony had the king of Armenia, wearing golden chains, led through the city in a procession to the Temple of Sarapis. He himself had taken up the role of Dionysus again, with his hair bound with ivy, riding in a special chariot and holding a sacred wand in his hand. Money and food were distributed in the streets in this extravagant ceremony, which was later called a triumph by Antony's enemy Octavian. In fact, it was no such thing, though certain parts of the

M. ANTONII VITA EX PLVTARCHO PER LEO
NARDVM ARETINV TRADVCTA INCIPIT.
M. ANTONIVS
MARCI ANTONII
uitam multiplici ac uaria
historiarum serie contextam
& uel magnitudine rerum
uel mutabilitate fortunae
admirandam ad te Salu
tate in hoc libro mictimus
e graeco sermone in latino
traductam

Antony dressed as Dionysus, complete with a crown of ivy in his hair, as he paraded through the city's streets.

event must have been similar in style. The point of the accusation was that triumphs should only have been held in Rome, and only as part of a celebration held at the Temple of Jupiter. If this had been a triumph it would have been an illegal act, and one of terrible arrogance.

DRAMATIC ANNOUNCEMENTS

Shortly afterward, however, Cleopatra and Antony held another ceremony, a great public affair in the Gymnasium at Alexandria. Seated on a raised silver platform, on golden thrones with their children below them, they made a series of pronouncements about their kingdoms. First Antony spoke about Caesar, and then proclaimed that he was dividing up the kingdoms of the eastern empire. Caesarion, now aged 13, was Caesar's true son and would become king of kings, subordinate only to his mother, who would be queen of kings and queen of her sons, the kings. Alexander Helios, six, would become king of Armenia, Media, and all lands to the east all the way to India, which was taken to mean the Parthian lands that still had to be overcome. Cleopatra Selene, also six, was given Cyrenaica and

Crete, while the baby, Ptolemy Philadelphus, two, became king of Syria, overlord of all the kings of Asia and king of the lands recently acquired by his mother. This grand event described here is normally referred to as the Donations of Alexandria, and it would have dramatic consequences for both lovers once their Roman enemies heard about it.

Cleopatra had wanted the Donations because they offered her a chance to establish exactly the kind of working relationship with Rome that she wanted. She was willing to pay the Roman armies and support Roman causes if the Ptolemy dynasty benefited from it. Like her father before her, she realized that the Romans were in charge and that Egypt could coexist with Rome only in a subordinate role. Otherwise, it would be swallowed up into the giant empire. Her actions were later portrayed as threatening to Rome itself, as if she had some terrible ambition to rule from there.

In fact, Antony made it quite clear at all times that he was the supreme commander of Rome's eastern armies and that he would remain in control, no matter what else occurred. It is fairly certain that he loved Cleopatra deeply at this point, but his actions were not reckless. He saw shared rule by

Greeks and Romans as a good model for stability in the region, and saw no need to insist on Roman dominance.

In spite of this, coins minted at this time show Marc Antony with his son Antyllus, making clear that his Roman child by his Roman wife Fulvia was still his real heir. This perception was important to him in Rome, where Octavian's supporters were busy trying to blacken his name.

ACCUSATIONS AND CONFLICT

After the Donations, Antony and Cleopatra resumed their turbulent life in the palace at Alexandria, where lavish extravagance was common. They were accused in Rome of drunkenness and perversion. Octavian accused them of adultery and lust, but in early 33 BCE Antony wrote to him saying that this should come as no surprise, as Cleopatra was his wife.

This letter is confusing, because Antony knew that he could not be legally married to Cleopatra for two reasons: he was already married to Octavia, and Roman law would not recognize any marriage to a foreigner.

Vivien Leigh and Lawrence Olivier portray the tumultuous romance between Antony and Cleopatra in Shakespeare's play of the same name as performed on Broadway.

Antony went on to say that he knew full well that Octavian himself was enjoying adulterous relationships with other women, and he saw this as no crime, so it may be that his statement about his marriage to Cleopatra was meant in a sarcastic sense. His genuine love for the queen seems the best explanation for what happened afterward. Whether Cleopatra loved him is also hard to gauge, but her destiny was bound ever closer to him and it is hard to believe she did not love him, despite her ruthless ambition to protect her country and its people.

During the summer of 33 BCE, Octavian and Antony came into further conflict with each other as it became obvious that civil war was looming. Antony knew that with Cleopatra's wealth he could amass huge armies and that he was the more experienced general, with a long record of success behind him. He claimed that the victory at Philippi over Caesar's assassins had been his and that Octavian had failed in the battle.

Antony repeated all kinds of slurs about Octavian, accusing him of failing to divide territories fairly with him, such as North Africa, taken from Lepidus, whom Octavian had demoted from the rank of triumvir without consultation. Octavian had behaved illegally with regard to himself as fellow triumvir and unconstitutionally at Rome, Antony claimed, failing to grant land for Antony's veteran soldiers to retire to in Italy.

In reply to this, Octavian launched a series of attacks on Antony and Cleopatra together. Antony was accused of sitting on a golden toilet seat, enslaved to the harlot queen, whose design was to rule Rome. He would share North Africa when Antony shared Armenia.

Antony could give his soldiers retirement land where he had made new conquests. In the meantime, Octavian demanded, Antony should stop giving Roman lands away for foreigners to rule and start behaving like a Roman governor. Such charges and accusations were made before the final conflict. The Egyptian queen's name had become a byword for ambition, lust, and treachery in Octavian's propaganda campaign.

THREATS OF ANOTHER WAR

Antony embarked on another campaign in the east, aiming to secure control over Media. But by Octo-

FALSE WORDS ABOUT A WILL?

On Plancus's return to Rome he spoke in hostile terms to the Senate about his former friends and gave information to Octavian about Antony's will, which had supposedly been left in the Temple of Vest at Rome. Octavian then committed the highly illegal act of compelling the chief vestal virgin to hand over the will. He studied the will alone and then made parts of it public. It said that Caesarion was indeed the true son of Julius Caesar, that Antony wanted his children by Cleopatra to inherit parts of his estate, and that he wanted on his death to be carried through the Forum in Rome before being taken to Alexandria for burial.

The first claim here was potentially damaging to Octavian as Caesar's heir, whereas the second claim indicated that Antony was living outside Roman law. The third claim, however, clearly showed that Antony saw himself as a man of the East. Octavian said that Antony was Cleopatra's puppet and that their shared design was to rule the empire from Alexandria, not Rome. All these supposed claims were probably made up by Octavian, and even the will itself may have been invented. We will never know the truth of this.

ber of 33 BCE, it became clear that war was brewing in the west against Octavian. Antony returned to Ephesus and met Cleopatra there to prepare for war. He wrote to the Senate in Rome offering to resign his position if Octavian would do the same, and asking for his actions in the east to be officially ratified by the Senate.

At the start of the next year, 32 BCE, the two consuls in Rome were both supporters of Antony, and it seemed for a while that he might succeed in his plans. During the first month of the year, however, the consul in Rome was Gnaeus Domitius Ahenobarbus, who was too afraid to read Antony's requests out publicly in the Senate, as he thought that Cleopatra's name would damage the cause. Frightened off by Octavian's hate campaign, he left well enough alone until his colleague Gaius Sosius took the chair in February. Sosius proposed a motion of criticism of Octavian, but this was stopped by a tribune acting on Octavian's orders. The tribune produced written evidence showing that Antony was acting illegally.

In this way Octavian made it impossible for the Senate to carry on its duties. Three hundred senators left Rome and went over to Antony, while

Octavian publicly congratulated himself for allowing them to leave in peace. This meant that there was no longer any effective political opposition to him in Rome. All of the parties involved had come to the point of no return, underlined a few months later when Antony divorced Octavia, the last link holding him to her brother and the last barrier between himself and Cleopatra.

After Antony's divorce from Octavia he too lost some of his supporters. Two men in particular changed sides and went over to Octavian in Rome: Marcus Titius and his uncle, Lucius Munatius Plancus. They had been friends of Cleopatra and staunch supporters of Antony up to this point. They may have changed sides thinking that Antony and Cleopatra were incapable of beating their enemy, or perhaps Cleopatra had insulted them.

CLEOPATRA CAUSES CONFLICT

Now Cleopatra's presence began to disturb some of Antony's leading advisors. Gnaeus Domitius Ahenobarbus, who had feared to speak out against Octavian while consul in Rome, now repeatedly urged his master to send Cleopatra back to Egypt, as she was damaging to the Roman cause. She must have felt increasingly under attack and isolated, though Antony's general Publius Canidius Crassus took her side. Crassus said that she had as much right and more to be part of the force, and that she had wider experience of command than many of the others present. She continued to stick close to Antony, on whom she relied heavily. His loyalty was encouraged by her gift of 200 ships, 20,000 talents, and supplies.

In April of 32 BCE, Antony and Cleopatra came to the Greek island of Samos, where they held a great festival in honor of Dionysus. The late-night parties and the wild festivities, together with the calling together of large numbers of actors from all across Greece, were yet one more lavish display of the Egyptian queen's wealth. Antony must have discussed invading Italy to catch Octavian unprepared, but she knew that her influence with him depended on the presence of her ships and her money, and she must have been reluctant to embark on a land war in Italy where she could not call the shots. He in turn may have been afraid to march on his own country, knowing that this would make him widely unpopular.

After Samos they sailed west to Athens, where Gaius Geminus, a friend of Antony from Rome, came to tell him that he must rid himself of Cleopatra. She treated Geminus badly, even threatening torture, and he went on his way. Antony seemed too drunk to care. He summoned his son Antyllus from Rome, who would stay by the couple's side in what was to come.

Octavian did not want to be accused of starting a civil war, so he declared war on Cleopatra, not on Antony, in the summer of 32 BCE. The two lovers took up their station at Patrae, modern Patras in Greece, as their forces were spread along the west coast of Greece. For some months there was considerable jostling, as Antony planned to block Octavian's ships on their way to Greece. Octavian's leading general, Marcus Vipsanius Agrippa, assessed the situation and began to break down Antony's defenses one by one.

The naval battle at Actium on September 2, 31 BCE, turned out to be the concluding conflict. When she failed to manage a decisive victory, Cleopatra withdrew her 60 ships from the battle lines. But this was no spur-of-the-moment escape. On board she had several things that were unusual for a ship sim-

Anthony and Cleopatra at the Battle of Actium, as depicted by Johann Georg Platzer. The battled occurred on September 2, 31 BCE.

ply going to battle: her treasure and her sails. Clearly, this escape was planned all along, possibly with the intention to reorganize her forces and fight elsewhere. Antony spotted her ships fleeing at full-speed and followed her. The lovers were headed for disaster.

CHAPTER 6

ALWAYS A QUEEN

Cleopatra insisted that she and Antony should fight by sea, thus at least in part instigating the clash at Actium. (Antony's generals urged him to fight by land.) General Canidius Crassus maintained his loyalty to Antony and later joined him, but Antony soon learned that his vast land armies were convinced to join Octavian. He may have fallen into a deep depression and lamented his decision to ignore his advisors as they sailed south to Egypt.

When they both arrived in Egypt, Antony remained at the port of Paraetonium, on the border with Cyrenaica, in case Octavian might be behind him, while the queen made her way to Alexandria. On her arrival, Cleopatra decked the bows of her ships with trophies and pretended to have won a great victory, in case her people should rise up

Cleopatra, During the Battle of Actium, in which she may have insisted Antony participate, against the wishes of his advisors.

against her in protest for her losing the war. She had several leading Alexandrians killed, and she hoarded together all the money and treasure she could, the best protection she could still muster.

FEELING THE BREATH OF DISASTER

When Antony returned to Alexandria, he lived for a short time alone near the Pharos lighthouse, staying out of Cleopatra's way. She may even have been grateful for this, as she knew she could easily lose the confidence of her own people now. After a short time, however, he left his retreat and rejoined the queen. They formed a drinking club called the Order of the Inseparable in Death and started on another round of late-night parties. Caesarion, now about 16, was enrolled into the list of adults, while Antyllus, Antony's son by Fulvia, was given the man's toga to wear for the first time. Cleopatra's coruler and Antony's heir were now both accepted as men, one of them Greek, the other Roman. Soon, however, Cleopatra began to fear for Caesarion's safety, and she tried to send him away. She feared for her own future, too, and had a squadron of ships transported across the neck of land leading to the Red Sea, so she might escape from Egypt to the East. However, the Nabataean Arabs, local inhabitants who had become hostile to Cleopatra and Antony when they were deprived of their right to collect bitumen on the Dead Sea, set fire to the ships before they could be used.

Octavian did not come immediately to Egypt, though his arrival there was clearly just a matter of time. Not only did Octavian need to crush his rival, he needed the Egypt's wealth to pay his soldiers. By the summer of 30 BCE, he was present in Samos and Rhodes, where he confirmed the deal with Herod over Judea. Cleopatra had no allies left, and her enemies were now all close to Octavian, who took up position at Ptolemais Ace. She felt the breath of disaster and sent a message to Octavian offering her abdication, provided that her children could rule in her place. Antony also sent a message to his enemy through his son Antyllus. Money was offered, and Antony said he would retire. Cleopatra offered more money. Octavian kept the money, but to all these approaches he remained impassive, knowing that he was on the point of complete victory. His only reaction to

Cleopatra was an offer that he would agree to any reasonable terms if she had Antony exiled from Egypt or killed. He sent a messenger called Thyrsus to discuss terms with her, but Antony had him flogged.

Hearing that the enemy had taken the port of Pelusium, Cleopatra became enraged and commanded that the wife and children of its commander Seleucus should be put to death. She began to assemble all her valuables and treasure in her own mausoleum, together with firewood. She knew the monument could be sealed off, and the presence of the firewood might encourage Octavian to think twice before attacking her and watching her treasure go up in flames. As Octavian got nearer, Antony led a cavalry charge against the approaching troops and scored his final victory, successfully driving them back. Yet within days, by August 1, 30 BCE, most of his soldiers had deserted him. This was the day that Octavian would later celebrate as the real moment of his victory. Later, he even named the month of August after himself to commemorate the event, though this was years later, after he had first renamed himself Augustus. At a party late at night, Antony and his friends heard strange sounds, as if a group of partygoers were noisily leaving the city, going out through the gate that led toward Octavian's troops. It was said by some that the sound was made by the gods who were leaving, abandoning Antony and Cleopatra.

A message came from the Mausoleum to Antony, saying that the queen was dead. This may have been just another part of the confusion that followed, or it may have been Cleopatra's deliberate attempt to drive Antony to suicide before trying to reach her own settlement with the conquering forces of Octavian. We cannot know the truth, but the effect on Antony was immediate. He stabbed himself in the chest with a dagger. As he lay dying he was brought to the Mausoleum, where his body had to be lifted up through a window. Cleopatra called him husband, lord, and emperor, and then she gave him wine. Antony died and she set about embalming his body herself.

It is unclear how Cleopatra died herself, though various accounts say she may have met Octavian first. Did she try to captivate him, as she had done before with Caesar and Antony? This seems unlikely. She had beaten and torn at her hair and breasts in mourning for Antony, and her

The Death of Cleopatra, as illustrated by Alessandro Turchi. When Antony found out, he reportedly stabbed himself with a dagger.

appearance must have indicated her grief. At 39 years of age, she was older than the 33-year-old Octavian, who loved his wife, Livia, and was in any case far too focused to let such a distraction affect his plans. He did not want responsibility for her death, but must have been delighted when he found out she had killed herself. Her attendants Iras and Charmian were found with her body, and the last words of Charmian were, "It is well done indeed and fitting for a princess descended of so many royal kings."

The story that she was killed by an asp, a type of snake, is just one of a set of stories surrounding her death. Modern scientists believe that a cobra may have been rcsponsible rather than an asp, as her body was found in a state of peace that could have

Rather than a snake called an asp, as historically thought, modern scientists think that a cobra might have been the reptile responsible for Cleopatra's death.

come about from that sort of poison. The cobra was often used by the pharaohs as a symbol of their power, and this would be a fitting end for a queen who had always sought to protect her dynasty in Egypt. Cleopatra's body was not disfigured, apart from some marks on her arms, and she wore her royal robes. Octavian exploited her death in a later triumph, when a statue of her with a snake on it was paraded through the streets of Rome.

The queen's death marked the end of a remarkable life and the beginning of a new era for Egypt, which became a special sort of Roman province. It was too wealthy to be trusted to any ambitious Roman senator, and future emperors retained it as a personal possession, governed by special envoys. Cleopatra was the last of the Ptolemies and the last of the pharaohs. She was a highly intelligent woman who had learned many languages so she could talk directly to her subjects. It is believed that she spoke Greek, Egyptian, Hebrew, Troglodyte, Arabian, Syrian, Median, and even Parthian. She always stayed faithful to her father's idea that Egypt should be governed with Roman support, but now the West had prevailed over the East, and her empire was vanquished. Her name would be blackened in the

POST-CLEOPATRA

Alexander Helios and Ptolemy Philadelphus were taken to Rome and were marched through the streets in Octavian's triumph. They were then taken with their sister, Cleopatra Selene, to Mauretania, in modern Morocco. Later Cleopatra Selene became the wife of King Juba II of Mauretania.

Antyllus sought protection in the large Temple of Caesar in Alexandria, after his father Marc Antony's death. Octavian was afraid to let him live, however, in case Antony's supporters should use him later on as the focus for a rebellion. He was beheaded, betrayed by his own tutor, Theodorus.

Caesarion was caught trying to escape from Egypt and was killed, as Octavian feared his connection to Caesar and how this might encourage later supporters in Rome or Egypt to use him as a figurehead for a future rebellion.

The general Marcus Vipsanius Agrippa continued to serve Octavian for many years to come. He was considered the finest general of his day, and he married Octavian's daughter Julia. He died in 12 BCE.

Octavian became the first citizen of Rome after his final defeat of Antony and Cleopatra. In practice, this meant that he became the first of the emperors, establishing his constitutional authority in settlements reached in 27 BCE and 23 BCE. He adopted the name of Augustus, meaning the "respected one." He reigned successfully until his death in 14 BCE.

Elizabeth Taylor portrays Cleopatra, who has shouldered a reputation for all kinds of treachery, but she never wavered from her ultimate position: a queen.

future by the man who had caused her the greatest damage in life, Octavian, who also controlled a propaganda machine that systematically sought to destroy the good name of her lover Antony. Writers paid and supported by Octavian described her as a deadly monster, a menace to freedom, her mind corrupted by drink and delusion. She was perverted, cruel, lustful, and arrogant, a byword for seduction in future generations. So they said. Cleopatra may have been some of these things, but for most of her extraordinary life she remained fully conscious of who she was—a queen.

bitumen A thick, black asphalt that occurs naturally and was used as cement or mortar in Asia Minor.

consul The title given to a senior Roman magistrate, a man who had reached the top of the *cursus honorum*. There were always two consuls chosen at any one time, in theory so one could overrule the other. The office is the equivalent in modern-day terms of a prime minister or president.

diadem A crown or headband with jewels.

dynasty A period of rule where the kings and queens of a land all come from the same family.

envoy Someone who works to deliver messages or act as a representative.

eunuch A castrated man.

Forum The center of Rome, which consisted of many public buildings, including temples, shops, and law courts.

garrison A group of soldiers who stay in a town for the purpose of defending it.

gymnasium An area where athletes would train or perform. The Gymnasium at Alexandria was a huge colonnaded public building.

Macedonia A large area in the north of Greece, extending into the neighboring countries of Yugoslavia and Bulgaria. Its people considered themselves to be Greek, though not all the other Greeks agreed with them. Its foremost king was Alexander the Great, who died in 323 BCE after amassing a huge empire.

republic This term is often used of the Roman state, represented by the acronym SPQR, meaning the Senate and People of Rome. After Augustus became the first emperor of Rome, the republic was in effect an empire controlled by one man, but the illusion was maintained that the republic still existed and that the Senate and people were as important as they had always been in Rome's early history. Republic literally means "public thing."

Senate Body of about 600 senior statesmen, whose authority combined with the emperor's. It acted as the lawgiver of Rome and its importance in Roman history cannot be overestimated.

signet ring A ring engraved with a design or letters, such as one's initials.

squadron A group of military made up of soldiers, ships, or aircraft.

toga A woolen garment worn by Romans. A ceremony took place when a boy reached the age of around 14, when he put on a man's toga for the first time—a big event in a young man's life.

tribune An official whose original job was to defend the people of Rome from exploitation by the rich and powerful. A tribune had the right of veto to block discussions taking place in government.

triumph A victory parade in which a Roman general would celebrate a victory in war by leading a procession through the streets of Rome. The people of the city would attend in large numbers, and gifts of money or grain would be handed out as part of the event.

triumvirate A group of three men who assumed the rule of the Roman state. The first triumvirate was formed in 60 BCE by Pompey the Great, Julius Caesar, and Marcus Licinius Crassus. The second triumvirate was formed in 43 BCE by Mark Antony, Octavian, and Marcus Aemilius Lepidus.

American Research Center in Egypt (U.S. Office)
8700 Crownhill Blvd., Suite 507
San Antonio, Texas 78209-1130
(210) 821-7000
e-mail: info@arce.org
Website: http://www.arce.org
The American Research Center in Egypt (ARCE) supports education, training, and preservation of Egypt and its cultural heritage.

Archaeological Institute of America Headquarters
Boston University
656 Beacon Street, 6th Floor
Boston, MA 02215-2006
Email: aia@aia.bu.edu
Website: https://www.archaeological.org
The Archaeological Institute of America (AIA) is the oldest and largest group in North America that dedicates itself to all things archaeology.

California Classical Association—Northern Section
Attn: Gillian McIntosh, Treasurer
581 Frederick Street
San Francisco, CA 94117
Website: http://www.ccanorth.org/
The CCA encourages the instruction and training of Classics such as through conferences and relationships with other classical organizations.

The Classical Association of Canada
Department of Greek and Roman Studies
University of Victoria
Victoria, BC V8W 3P4
Canada
(250) 721-8528
Website: http://cac-scec.ca
This nonprofit organization was formed in 1947 to promote the study of Greek and Roman civilizations as well as how they affected later societies and modern culture.

WEBSITES

Because of the changing nature of internet links, Rosen Publishing has developed an online list of websites related to the subject of this book. This site is updated regularly. Please use this link to access the list:

http://www.rosenlinks.com/LANW/cleo

Amstutz, Lisa J. *Ancient Egypt* (Ancient Civilizations). North Mankato, MN: ABDO Publishing, 2015.

Cornell, Tim, and John Matthews. *Atlas of the Roman World.* Oxford, England: Phaidon, 1982.

Fleming, Fergus. *Ancient Egypt's Myths and Beliefs.* New York, NY: Rosen Young Adult, 2012.

Grant, Michael. *Cleopatra.* London: Phoenix Press, 1972.

Hollar, Sherman. *Ancient Egypt.* New York, NY: Britannica Educational Publishing, 2012.

Kuiper, Kathleen. *The 100 Most Influential Women of All Time.* New York: Britannica Educational Publishing, 2010.

Kuiper, Kathleen. *Ancient Egypt.* New York, NY: Britannica Educational Publishing, 2011.

Massie, A. *Antony.* London: Hodder and Stoughton, 1997.

Massie, A. *Augustus.* London: Hodder and Stoughton, 1986.

Nagle, Jeanne. *Top 101 Remarkable Women.* New York, NY: Britannica Educational Publishing, 2014.

Nardo, Don. *Cleopatra* (Influential Women). San Diego, CA: ReferencePoint Press, 2016.

Quie, Sarah. *Ancient Egyptian Civilization.* New York, NY: Rosen Central, 2010.

Shakespeare, William. *Antony and Cleopatra* (Dover Thrift Editions) Mineola, NY: Dover Publications, Inc., 2014.

Shea, Therese. *Discovering Egyptian Dynasties* (Exploring African Civilizations). New York, NY: Rosen Publishing, 2014.

Shecter, Vicky Alvear. *Cleopatra Rules! The Amazing Life of the Original Teen Queen.* Honesdale, PA: Boyds Mills

Press, 2013.

Staley, Erin. *Discovering Ancient Egypt*. New York, NY: Britannica Educational Publishing, 2015.

Wilding, Valerie. *Cleopatra: The Story of the Beautiful Egyptian Queen*. London, England: Bloomsbury Publishers, 2013.

Brown, Chris. "Cleopatra." *National Geographic*. July 2011. Retrieved May 20, 2016 (http://ngm.nationalgeographic.com/2011/07/cleopatra/brown-text).

Cook, S. A., et al. *The Cambridge Ancient History,* Volume X. Cambridge, England: Cambridge University Press, 1966.

Dio Cassius. *The Roman History*. London: Penguin, 1987.

Holbl, Gunther. *A History of the Ptolemaic Empire*. London: Routledge, 2001.

Hughes-Hallett, Lucy. *Cleopatra*. London: Pimlico, 1990.

Plutarch. *Makers of Rome*. London: Penguin, 1965.

Scullard, Hugh H. *From the Gracchi to Nero*. London: Methuen, 1959.

Talbert, Richard J. A. *Atlas of Classical History*. London: Routledge, 1985.

ABOUT THE AUTHORS

Zoe Lowery is an avid student of history, constantly reading and getting lost in the fascinating stories like that of Cicero. She has written and edited a number of history books for Rosen Publishing, Gareth Stevens Publishing, Enslow Publishing, and PowerKids Press. She enjoys a quiet afternoon in just about any library, but especially those near her home in Colorado.

Julian Morgan earned his B.A. in Greek studies at Bristol University, England, in 1979. He also earned a master's degree in computers and education at King's College, London, in 1990. He has been head of classics at Derby Grammar School. Julian has a special interest in software design and has published many programs, including ROMANA and Rome the Eternal City, through his business, J-PROGS. He is a member of the American Classical League's committee on educational computer applications. He is the computing coordinator for the Joint Association of Classical Teaching (JACT) and has a regular column, "Computanda," in their bulletin. He also runs a training business called Medusa, which specializes in helping teachers of classics to use information technology in their teaching.

PHOTO CREDITS

Cover, p. 3 DEA Picture Library/Getty Images; cover (background), pp. 54–55, 94–95 Heritage Images/Hulton Fine Art Collection/Getty Images; p. 7 DEA/S. Vannini/De Agostini/Getty Images; pp. 12–13, 27, 36–37, 72 Hulton Archive/Getty Images; p. 15 © Peter Hermes Furian/Alamy Stock Photo; p. 18 topnotch100/iStock/Thinkstock; p. 21 © www.BibleLandPictures.com/Alamy Stock Photo; pp. 24–25 Ancient Art & Architecture Collection Ltd./Alamy Stock Photo; pp. 32–33 © North Wind Picture Archives/Alamy Stock Photo; p. 41 © Lebrecht Music and Arts Photo Library/Alamy Stock Photo; p. 43 BMPix/iStock/Thinkstock; p. 46 © World History Archive/Alamy Stock Photo; pp. 50–51 Wolfgang Kaehler/LightRocket/Getty Images; pp. 52–53 © Heritage Image Partnership Ltd./Alamy Stock Photo; pp. 61, 74 DEA/A. Dagli Orti/De Agostini/Getty Images; p. 63 MariMarkina/iStock/Thinkstock; p. 66–67 Martha Holmes/The LIFE Images Collection/Getty Images; p 78 Cornell Capa/The LIFE Picture Collection/Getty Images; pp. 86–87 © V&A Images/Alamy Stock Photo; p. 89 Bob Thomas/Popperfoto/Getty Images; p. 96 Science & Society Picture Library/Getty Images; p. 99 Manchester Daily Express/SSPL/Getty Images; interior pages background images © iStockphoto.com/kikkalek5050 (sky), Triff/Shutterstock.com (map).

Designer: Brian Garvey; Editor: Heather Moore Niver; Photo Researcher: Heather Moore Niver